The First Noel

The
FIRST NOEL

ILLUSTRATED · BY · JODY · WHEELER

ideals children's books
Nashville, Tennessee

ISBN-13: 978-0-8249-5621-9

Published by Ideals Children's Books
An imprint of Ideals Publications
A Guideposts Company
Nashville, Tennessee
www.idealsbooks.com

Color separations by Precision Color Graphics, Franklin, Wisconsin
Printed and bound in China

Library of Congress CIP data on file

Leo_Jun10_1

Song arrangement by Dick Torrans, Melode, Inc.
Designed by Eve DeGrie

For Vanessa and Julien—J.W.

THE FIRST NOEL

THE FIRST NOEL first appeared in print in 1833, but it was handed down for many generations before it was published. It is thought that this carol was popular in seventeenth-century England, when church leaders did not allow their congregations to sing—only trained choirs could sing inside the church. The choirs' songs were most often somber chants with little melody.

Churchgoers took their singing voices outside, where they were joined by wandering minstrels who provided music. Together, they created joyful carols, like "The First Noel," and they made up circle dances to perform with the songs. At that time, the English word *carol* actually meant "a ring or circle dance." As time passed, *carol* came to refer to the song, rather than to the dance.

Historians cannot agree whether "The First Noel" originated in France or England, because the French word *noel* and English word *nowell* sound identical, and their long-ago meanings are not clear. Today, these two words mean exactly the same thing—a Christmas carol.

*T*he first *noel* the angel did say
was to certain poor shepherds
in fields as they lay,
in fields where they
lay keeping their sheep
on a cold winter's night
that was so deep.

They looked up and saw a star
shining in the east, beyond them far.
And to the earth it gave great light,
and so it continued
both day and night.

*A*nd by the light of that same star,
three wise men came from country far.

To seek for a king was their intent,
and to follow the star wherever it went.

This star drew nigh to the northwest;
o'er Bethlehem it took its rest.
And there it did both stop and stay,
right over the place where Jesus lay.

Then did they know assuredly
within that house
the king did lie;
one entered it them for to see
and found the babe
in poverty.

Then entered in

those wise men three,

full reverently upon the knee,

and offered there, in his presence,

their gold and myrrh

and frankincense.

*B*etween an ox stall and an ass,
this child, truly, there he was;

for want of clothing, they did him lay
all in the manger, among the hay.

Noel, noel, noel, noel.

Born is the king of Israel.

The FIRST NOEL

cold win - ter's night that was so deep.
so it con - tin - ued both day and night.
fol - low the star wher - ev - er it went.

No - el, no - el, no - el, no - el.

Born is the king of Is - ra - el.

4. This star drew nigh to the northwest;
o'er Bethlehem it took its rest.
And there it did both stop and stay,
right over the place where Jesus lay.

5. Then did they know assuredly
within that house the king did lie;
one entered it them for to see
and found the babe in poverty.

6. Then entered in those wise men three,
full reverently upon the knee,
and offered there, in his presence,
their gold and myrrh and frankincense.

7. Between an ox stall and an ass,
this child, truly, there he was;
for want of clothing, they did him lay
all in the manger, among the hay.

*A*nd, lo, the star, which they saw in the east,
went before them, till it came and
stood over where the young child was.
When they saw the star, they rejoiced
with exceeding great joy.

—MATTHEW 2:9B–10